howdy, word nerds!

about this study guide

Do you dream of winning a school spelling bee, or even attending the Scripps National Spelling Bee National Competition? *Words of the Champions* is the official study resource of the Scripps National Spelling Bee, so you've found the perfect place to start. Prepare for a 2023 or 2024 classroom, grade-level, school, district, county, regional or state spelling bee with this list of 4,000 words.

All words in this book have been selected by the Scripps National Spelling Bee from our official dictionary, Merriam-Webster Unabridged (http://unabridged.merriam-webster.com).

words of the
champions
. . . .
YOUR KEY TO THE BEE

Official Dictionary
of the
Scripps National
Spelling Bee

merriam-webster.com

Words of the Champions is divided into three difficulty levels, ranked One Bee, Two Bee and Three Bee. These are great words to challenge you, whether you're just getting started in spelling bees or if you've already participated in several. At the beginning of each level, you'll find the *School Spelling Bee Study List* words. For any classroom, grade-level or school spelling bee, study the 150-word One Bee *School Spelling Bee Study List*, the 150-word Two Bee *School Spelling Bee Study List* and the 150-word Three Bee *School Spelling Bee Study List*: a total of 450 words.

Following the *School Spelling Bee Study List* in each level, you'll find pages marked "Words of the Champions." Are you a school spelling bee champion or a speller advancing to compete beyond the school level? Study these pages to make sure you're prepared to do your best when these words are asked in the early rounds of competition. And remember, although spelling bees will start with words from this guide, they often end with words you haven't studied.

New this year, at the end of this study resource you'll find games, puzzles and themed lists to help you engage with the words in new ways. Enjoy!

Each year, the Scripps National Spelling Bee will release a new version of *Words of the Champions* featuring 800 new words, including an all-new *School Spelling Bee Study List*.

Your spelling bee journey starts now, and taking the first step toward becoming a star athlete of the English language makes you a Champion. These *Words* are for you.

about the Scripps National Spelling Bee

The Scripps National Spelling Bee is the nation's largest and longest-running educational program. By inspiring the exploration of words, the Scripps National Spelling Bee illuminates pathways to lifelong curiosity, celebrates academic achievement and enriches communities. Visit spellingbee.com for more information about the Bee and to check if your school is enrolled. The Scripps National Spelling Bee is administered on a not-for-profit basis by The E.W. Scripps Company.

table of
contents

word lists

vocab

fun

difficulty level: one bee

school spelling bee study list

The first, second and third-grade words from the 2024 School Spelling Bee Study List.

sky	heap	bedroom
wow	ladder	branch
hug	tug	letter
snap	spoon	spring
tape	spark	dance
sips	later	front
hard	hair	roast
why	open	brave
first	this	bright
tide	his	scream
bow	May	river
back	grid	bride
find	wag	stall
name	near	point
oops	zip	wedding
more	rug	little
toss	dots	doctor
chin	pat	peel
park	pole	snack
bike	snake	notebook
nest	mound	brain
rude	smaller	pride
deal	grand	dear
store	gross	live
roads	wish	tubes
cool	stove	cloth
wake	join	gazed
vase	state	mile
tune	enter	float
coat	blank	snail
four	give	second
block	other	drew

hug — verb - to put one's arms around and press tightly.

brain — noun - the portion of the central nervous system in vertebrates that makes up the organ of thought.

in good company

When it comes to spelling bee participants, the more the merrier! In fact, more than 11 million spellers participate each year in qualifying spelling bees throughout the country and around the world.

stood	corner
nagged	barely
scan	able
glue	present
ground	clearly
shower	really
endless	overcome
plunger	sketch
fireworks	evening
dazzle	again
climb	finally
April	thumbs
subway	glittery
broken	together
stew	while
shall	mother
flowers	worth
angry	solve
create	credit
drooped	steel
cluttered	pour
bursting	anybody
edge	whisper
glasses	Thursday
gently	music
crown	wears
shutters	thoughts

whisper — verb – to speak softly, especially with the aim of preserving secrecy.

Great Words, Great Works Reading Program

Each year, the Scripps National Spelling Bee publishes our School Spelling Bee Study List to help students prepare for classroom and school-level spelling bees. These words come from Great Words, Great Works, a list of books carefully selected by the Bee's editorial team. Find it at spellingbee.com/book-list.

difficulty level: one bee

Words of the Champions

Organized alphabetically, these words are a great place to start your journey to mastering *Words of the Champions*! Words with a single asterisk (*) indicate a primarily British spelling. Words with a double asterisk (**) are the preferred spelling. A complete list of the words that were added to this year's study list can be found on page 40.

A

abaft
abandon
abashed
abject
aboriginal
acceptance
acclaim
accolade
accomplice
acquit
acrostic
adage
addendum
addition
addle
adhesion
adjective
adjudicate
admonition
adnate
adsum
advection
adversaria
affront
aforesaid
afroth
agility
agitation
algae
alienate
alpaca — noun – a South American mammal that resembles a llama.
alpha
altercation
amass
Americana
amiably
Amish

amnesty
amulet
amusement
ancho
anime
animus
anklet
anniversary
annotate
anoint
ante
anthropology
anyway
apology
apparel
applicable
appraisal
apprehensive
arithmetic
armadillo
astonish
astounding
atomic
atonement
attendee
attitude
auction
auditorium
avalanche
avatar
avenue
aviation
awry

B

bachelorette
backgammon
badger

bailiff
ballad
banana
banquet
baptismal
barbie
bask
become
Bengal
bias
birdie
biscuit
bizarro
blandish
blarney
bleary
bleat
blemish
blink
blizzard
blooper
blurb
boarders
boogie-woogie
bootless
botany — noun – the science of plants.
bother
bountiful
bowie
breathtaking
brethren
brick
bristle
brochure
broil
bubbly
buffet
buffoonery

6

bumblebee
bungee
burial
buzzworthy

C
cabbage
cactus
cadence
calculator
calendar
camcorder
candid
canoe
canteen
cantor
capacity
capitalist
captivated
caramel
carnation
carnival
carriage
carrot
cashier
casino
casserole
casualty
caterpillar
cathedral
catnap
celebratory
celery
celestial
cello
cement
census
centipede
charioteer
charitable
chastise

chortle
chowder
churlish
chute**
　OR shute
cidery
cinderella
cinematic
citation
clarinet
classical
clearance
cleave
clover
clowder
coach
coalition
cockles
collie
collision
combustible
comedienne
commandeer
comparison
compass
compatriots
compelling
complementary
comportment
composite
conch ——— noun – an edible marine mollusk with a large spiral shell.
concrete
condemn
condensation
condiments
conference
consideration
contraction
contradictory
contrite
contusion

conundrum
convention
convocation
convoy
cooperate
copperhead
corgi
corkscrew
cornily
cranium
criminal
criteria
crocodile
crumpet
crux
curator
curfew
curio
cushion
cyclone
cymbals

D
daft
daisy
daresay
dawdle
debris
debunk
decor
definitely
delta
derby
designer
dialect
dicey
dictum
difficult
digression
dillydally
disaster

cruising the airwaves

The first broadcast of the Bee wasn't on television – it was on radio! It wasn't until 1946 that it was first televised.

disposition
disrepair
distinctive
diva
diverge
diversion
diversity
divine
divvy
docket
documentary
domino — ● noun – a small dotted slab that together with other such slabs is used to play a game.
donatee
downcast
dragoon
dramatization
dreadlocks
dribbles
drivel
Dudley
dumbwaiter
duress
dynamite

E
eagerly
earmark
earnestly
eclipse
editorial
eerily
effortless
Egyptian
eighth
Einstein
elaborative
elasticity
elegant
element
elevator
elicitation
eligibility
ellipse
elocution
elucidate
elusive — ● adjective – hard to catch.

emancipatory
embassy
embezzlement
emblazoned
emerald
empty
encore
encroach
endearing
endure
enervate
engineer
entreat
entrée
entrepreneur
enumerated
enviable
epoxy
erode
eruption
escalator
escapade
essential
establishment
evaluate
evaporation
ewe
exaggerate
excursion
exemplar
exercise
existence
explode
extensive
extinct
extinguish
extracurricular
extradition
extraordinaire
exude

F
fabulist
facade
factorial
fadeaway

fallacy
fanatic
fashionista
feeble
fellowship
felonious
ferret
fervently
fez
fido
fie
filar
filbert
financier
fission
fisticuffs
flabbergast
flashback
flattery
fleeciness
fleetness
flexitarian
flight
flimflammer
flipperling — ● noun – a small animal with broad flat limbs adapted for swimming (as a baby seal).
floridly
flounder
flourish
flout
fluctuation
fluid
flummery
foible
folate
folly
fomentation
foosball
foothills
foozle
foppery
forensics
forfeit
forgeable
formalize
    OR formalise*
fortification

frailty

freckle

freegan

freight

fribble

frisket

frock

frontier

frugal

fundamental

funnel

furnace

futility

G

gab

gaffer

gaggle

gallant

galley

gardenesque

gargle

garniture

gaucho

gazette

genius

genteel

ghastly

giggle ———● verb – to laugh in a silly manner.

gist

gizzard

glitterati

gnarled

Godspeed

goober

gossip

gotcha

gouge

graham

grandeur

graphologist

grapple

gridiron

griefful

groom

gruel

guess

gymnastics

H

habitual

haggle

hamlet

handle

handyman

hangar

haphazard

hardtack

harmonious

harrowing

hatchet

hazelnut

headlong

heavenly

heiress

heist

hermitage

hexagonal

Highlands

hijab

hoagies

hoax

hobble

hollyhock

homage

homesteader

homicide

honeybee

horseradish

hostile

howler

hurriedly

husk ———● noun – one of the leaves enveloping an ear of corn.

hydra

hydrant

I

iceberg

ignite ———● verb – to set on fire.

inclusion

income

infiltrate

infirm

inflammable

influential

inglorious

insomnia

installation

intellectual

intensify

intertidal

intricate

irrigation

irritability

island

isms

isolation

J

jammer

jankers

jersey ———● noun – a soft knitted fabric used for making clothing, especially sportswear.

jitterbug

joinery

junior

K

kazoo

kennel

kenning

why is it so hard to spell English words?

English consists of originally English words, but it also collected words from other languages and made them part of the English lexicon. With 26 letters and about 44 letter sounds, English is a hodgepodge of letters and sounds that don't always line up. Take the letter 'x,' for example, found in the words "extra," "mix," and "example," or the vowel sound in "weigh" and "way"!

kernel

kilt

kindred

kiwi

knight

knoll

kodak

kudos —• noun – praise given for some achievement.

L

labradoodle

lactose

languish

lapel

lateral

lawyer

league

leaven

leeway

legacy

legislature

legitimately

leisure

lettuce

lexicon

liege

ligament

likelier

limelight —• noun – the center of public attention.

linguistics

literally

livid

lucky

lumbar

luminance

lupine

M

macaw

macrobiotics

madrigal

magician

mahogany

maidenhair

maize

mambo

manacle

mandate

manta

mantra

marathon

maritime —• adjective – of or relating to navigation or commerce on the sea.

marooned

martial

mastiff

maternity

matrimony

mauve

maverick

maximum

mayhem

measly

medallion

melody

melted

membership

memes

memorandum

menial

merchandise

merely

Merlin

meteor

metrical

Michigander

millionaire

mince

minutia

miraculous

mischief

misconception

missile

missive

mister

mockery

modality

modem

modify

modular

mogul

molasses

molecule

monopolize

    OR monopolise*

montage

moped

morose

mosaic

mummified

munchkin

musings

mutter

N

nationalism

neaten

necessity

neigh

nerfing

nervily

newbie

nocturnal

nominee

nonconformist

nozzles

nuggets —• plural noun – small usually round-shaped pieces of food.

O

obliterate

oblong —• adjective – having a shape that is elongated beyond a square or circle.

obscure

occupancy

olympiad

omega

omission

onion

optician

optimum

opulent

oracle

orchestra

ordinance

organelle

ounce

ouster

overtures

overweening

owlishly

ozone

P

pageantry
paginate
paisley
palatial
pallor
pantheon
parkour
parley
partridge —● noun – a medium-sized, short-winged game bird with short legs and neck.
passage
pastime
pathogen
patience
patrician
pauper
pear
peat
peddle
pedicure
pedigree
pending
penguin
peninsular
peony
performance
permafrost
peruse
pervasive
photogenic
physical
physicists
pillor
pitiful
placards
placate
platinum
platoon
pliant
plummet
portrait

praise
precursor
predicament
premonition
primitive
principality
prism
procedure
procrastinate
profiteer
prominent
prone
proposal
propulsion
prosperous
proxy
publish
puckish
pulpit
punctuation
pungent
punily
puniness
purification
puritan
purse
putrid
puzzles
pyramid

Q

quantify
quart
quaver
quirky —● adjective – full of peculiarities.
quota

R

rabid
raisin
rebuff

recanted
reconsider
recovery
recruit
redemption
reflect
regiment
registrar
rehearsal
reign
reiterate
rejuvenate
remorseful
renewable
replete
residue
respite
restive —● adjective – marked by fidgety or uneasy behavior.
retorts
retriever
revelation
revulsive
riddance
riffraff
riviera
rocket
row
rubric
rugby
rumor
    OR rumour*

S

sacrifice
salivate —● verb – to produce an excessive amount of drool.
sandal
satchel
scalp
scandal
scanty
scent

---

our mission:
By inspiring the exploration of words, the Scripps National Spelling Bee illuminates pathways to lifelong curiosity, celebrates academic achievement and enriches communities.

11

scholarship	soprano	**T**
science	sorbet	talent
sci-fi	spangled	tango
scooter	spatula	tase
scornfully	specificity	tawny
scrapple	spectral	technician
screeno	speculate	teenagers
scripture	spindle	tendency
scrooge	spiteful	terrier
scrounge	splurge	thawed
scrutiny	spreadsheet	thespian
scullery	sprite	thicket
sculpture	spry	thievery
seclusion	squeamish	thorn
seize	squirm	thrift
selfie	stagestruck	throughout
seller	stamina	tickled
semester	stampede	timber
sensory	stance	toastmaster
September	standee	toilsome
sequel	steampunk	transcription
serenade	stencil	transference
servitude	stereotypical	traverse
sewage	sterling	treasury
shaggy	sternum	treatise
shamrock	steroid	trendy
shindig	stewardship	trespass
shipping	stomach	trifle
shore	storm	trinkets
simmer	stowaway	troll
sister	strong	tropical
situation	stubble	trounce
skimmed	stupefy	trove
skirmish	substitute	truffle
skydiving	suffix	truly
slab	suitable	trumpet
sloop	summary	truncate
slovenly	sunflower	tubers
slurry	sunseeker	tunnel
snitch	surly	tutorial
sodden	surplus	twilight
solicit	swannery	
solidity	sweltering	**U**
solitude	sword	uncle
solstice	sympathy	undercroft
solvency	system	undergird

noun – a brass instrument with a flared bell and three buttons pressed to make different notes.

unfazed

unfurl

university

uppercut

urgency

useful

usher —● noun – someone who escorts people to seats at a gathering.

V

various

varnish

varsity

vascular

vassal

vault

veered

venue

versatile

version

vicinity —● noun – neighborhood.

vindictive

vinegar

vineyard

virtually

visibility

vlogging

vocabulary

volcano

votive

W

waiver

wamble

wand

warning

wasp

water

wattage

weald

wealthy

weaponry

welding

welterweight

wharf

wheedle

whelp

whereas

whet

whey

whimsical

whirlybird

whisk

wield

wimple

wince

windbaggery —● noun – pompous meaningless talk.

wizened

wordmonger

wring

Y

yammer —● verb – to talk rapidly, for a long time, and often loudly.

yawl

yeanling

yippee

yonder

yoo-hoo

yore

Z

zither —● noun – an instrument that has a shallow horizontal soundboard topped with 30 to 40 strings that are typically plucked by a performer.

a big-time Spellebrity

If you've watched the Bee before, you've probably seen his face. You've definitely heard his voice. We're talking about the head pronouncer of the Bee, Dr. Jacques Bailly. He won the Scripps National Spelling Bee in 1980 and took up the role of head pronouncer in 2003.

difficulty level: two bee

school spelling bee study list

The fourth, fifth and sixth-grade words from the 2024 School Spelling Bee Study List. Words with a single asterisk (*) indicate a primarily British spelling. Words with a double asterisk (**) are the preferred spelling.

bronze	pouch	ambush
flea	outfits	squire
buckeye	sewing	submerged
sudsy	transform	saucer
antlers ●→ *plural noun – horns of animals of the deer family, typically present only in the male.*	marble	gloaming ●→ *noun – twilight : dusk.*
dapper	gallon	engulf
stroll	flitting	graduate
cress	plaza	fascinated
bestie	yesterday	composition
cereal	nighttime	wisdom
silence	putty	ourselves
fury	glumly	invisible
howdy	ignore	completely
important	improve	poisonous
popovers	Internet	intimidate
thousand	pantry	drawers
razor	hungrily	disdain
roughly	confident	deliberately
drawl	vision	spacious
oddity	diamond	forearms
insult	stitchery	gratitude
valley	fiddlehead	appreciation
gather	hobbit	devotion
dessert	doughnut	inscription
stagecoach	OR donut	inventory
peaceful	precious	wheezy
ailment	wafting	possible
combat	occupy	replace
rotten	Afrobeat	crookedly
expressway	termite	fragrant
practice**	insulation	fowl
OR practise	intertwine	responsible
squash	recital	awfully
amused	furniture	manual

who knew?

The Scripps National Spelling Bee is the nation's largest and longest-running educational program.

thorax

tostones

bunions

bamboozled

Oman

flummox**

   OR flummix

   OR flummux

inscrutable

serenity

congregation

sentinel

Arctic

fluke

captain

delegation

verve

Vaseline

gastritis

platypus

salute

mantel

  OR mantle

amphitheater

desecration

diode

mischievous

bionic

syllables

sultanate

turban ———●

sausage

disgruntled

terrify

quip

information

incubator

droll

vultures

Arabic

Brooklyn

sacred

reindeer

disclaimer

quotation

superior

privilege

fallow

replica

provision

reference

havens

voracious

noun – a headdress consisting of a long cloth that is wrapped around a cap or directly around the head.

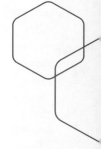

from around the world

Most spellers at the Scripps National Spelling Bee are from the United States, but spellers also come from Guam, Puerto Rico, the U.S. Virgin Islands, the Bahamas, Canada, Ghana and Department of Defense Schools in Europe.

difficulty level: two bee

Words of the Champions

Organized alphabetically, these words are a great place to continue your journey to mastering *Words of the Champions*! Words with a single asterisk (*) indicate a primarily British spelling. Words with a double asterisk (**) are the preferred spelling. A complete list of the words that were added to this year's study list can be found on page 40.

A

aardvark
aberration
ablation
ablaut
abnegation
abominable
abrogate
absolution
abstemious
academese
Acadians
accentuate
accrual
accumulate
acerbity
achromatic
acoustic
acquiesce
acral
acuity
acumen
acupuncture
adjugate
adjure
adolescence
adulation
advocatory
aerobics
affable
affeer
affenpinscher
affianced
affiliate

affluent
affogato
afghan
aficionado**
   OR afficionado
agalma
agate
agave
agelicism
aggrandizement
aglossal
agnail
agonistic
agoraphobia
aioli ——● noun – garlic mayonnaise.
akimbo
albeit
alimentation
allergenic
allocable
allonym
alluvial
alma mater
alpestrine
althorn
amalgam
ambrosial
ammonite
ammunition
amygdala
anabolic
anaglyphy
analects
analepsis

analgesia
anchorage
ancillary
anemic**
   OR anaemic
anent
anglophile
anhinga
anicca
anionic
anise
ankh
anneal
annuity
annulment
anodyne
anonymity
anorak
anserine
antacid
antagonistic
anticipatory
antipathy
antiquarian
antithesis
anxiety
aperture
apiary
aporia
apothecary
apotheosis
apparatus
approbatory
aqueduct

did you know?

Vocabulary questions were first introduced as part of the Bee on the written test in 2013. Oral vocabulary questions were given at the National Competition for the first time in 2021.

aqueous	augment	biomimicry
aquiclude	auklet	bittern
arbitrary	aureole	blastema
arboretum	auricular	blastogenesis
archaism	aurora	blatant
archetype	auspices	bloviate
arduous	austere	bodega
argot	avarice	bodkin
arietta	avifauna	boffin
armaments	avuncular	bona fide
armature		bonobo
armistice	**B**	bonsai
arpeggio	bacteriolytic	boomslang
arraign	ballyhooed	boondoggle
arrearage	balsamic	borough
art brut	bandicoot	bouffant —● adjective – voluminous.
artesian	bango	bowsprit
artifice	bariatrics	braille
asado	baronetcy	Brandywine
ascension	basilica	bravado
ascetic	bastion	breviloquence
Asgard	Bavarian cream	bric-a-brac
Asiago	beatific	Brigadoon
aspish	beguile	Broccolini
assailant	Belgravia	brockage
assiduous	Bellatrix	brogue
assumption	bellwether	bromide
assure	beneficent	brontophobia
asthmatic	benison	bruja
astral	bereavement	bruxism
astringent	beret	bubonic
astrobleme	bermudas	bucatini
astronaut	beseech	buffa
Astur	besieged	bulgogi
asylum	besmirch	bulgur**
ataxia	bethesda	OR bulghur
Aten	bibliopegist	bulwark
atlatl	bicameral	bumptious
atrabilious	bifurcate	Bundt
atresia	bilaterian	buoyancy
attaché	bilbo	bureau
attributive	billabong	burglarious
attrition	billiards	burgoo
aubergine	billingsgate	busby
auburn	biltong	
aughts	binomial	

C

cabaret

cadge

caducity

caffeine

caftan
   OR kaftan

calcify

callow

calumet

cambio

cameist

campanology

cancion

candelabrum

cannoli

cantankerous ➝● adjective – grumpy and argumentative.

capillary

capnometer

capstan

capsule

carbohydrates

carcinogenic

cardoon

caricature

carnage

carnitas

carnitine

cartilage

Cassandra

cassock

castellated

castigate

Castilian

castor

cataclysmic

catalepsy

catalina

catalyst

cathect

cathode

cattalo
   OR catalo

caudex

causal

caustic

cauterize

cavalcade

cayenne

cellophane

Celsius

cenotaph

centenary

cerebellum

cetology

chamberlain

chancellor

chaperonage

charcuterie

charismatic

château

chemise

Cheshire cat

chevalier

chide

Chihuahua

chimera
   OR chimaera*

chinook

chintzy

cholera

cholesterol

chrysalis

chrysolite

chupacabra

churchianity

churros

ciao

cicada

Cincinnati

circadian

circuitous

circumflex

civet

cladistics

clairvoyance

clandestine

clavichord

clemency

cloture

coalescence

coaxation

codswallop

coercive

coeval

cogently

cogitation

cognizant
   OR cognisant*

cohesive

cohosh

coiffure

colic

collectanea

collegiality

colocate

comanchero

comminatory

commiserative

commissioner

commodious

compendium

con forza

concision

conclave

concordance

conduit

Conestoga

confabulation

congeniality

conglutinant

connivery

consecrate

adjectives vs. nouns

"*My word ends with an /us/ sound! How do I know which letters to use?!*"
Here's a hint: Ask for the part of speech. If it's a noun, try -us; if it's an adjective, -ous is a safe bet.

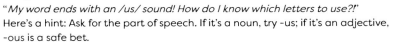

consequent
constabulary
consternation
constituent
consul
contemptuous
continuum
contrariwise
contrivance
contumelious
Coptic
cordillera
corduroy
coriander
Corinthian
corm
cornea
cornel
cornucopia
corollary
coroner
corpulent
corral
corrosive
corsage
cortex
cozen
credence
credulity
creel
crepuscular
crescive
cribbage
cribble
cribo
crinoline
crith
cruciferous
crustaceans
cryogenic
cudgel
cum laude
cumbersome
cumulus
curmudgeon
cutis

cyanosis
cybernetics
cygnet
cynicism

D

dactylic
Dalmatian
dandle
danseur
danta
darnel
davenport
deathin
debilitate
debutante
deceitful
deceleron
decennial
deciduous
decimation
declamatory
declension
declination
decurion
defiant
deglaciation
déjà vu**
   déjà vue
delectable
deleterious
deliquesce
deltoidal
dementia
demerits
demographics
demonstrative
demulcent
denominator
denticulate
depose
depravity
depreciate
depredation
deprivation
derelict

derisive
deserter
desertification
desolate
desultorily
detritus
deuterium
diacritic
diadem
dialysis
Dianthus
diaspora
diathermy
diatonic
dietetic
dihedral
dilapidated
diligence
diluent
dimorphism
dirigible
discombobulate
discomfiture
discountenance
discreetly
discretionary
disembogue
disjunct
Disneyfication
disparate
disproportionate
dissemble
dissipate
dissonance
distraught
divestiture
dodecahedron
dogana
doldrums
dolma
dolmen
domesticity
domiciled
domineering
dopamine
Dorking

dowager

dowdy

dromic ——●   adjective – of, relating to, or in the form of a racecourse.

druid

drumlin

drupiferous

du jour

duchy

duplicitous

durango

dysgraphia

dyspeptic

dystopia

E

ebullience

ectoplasm

eczema

Edenic

educand

efface

effervescent

efflux

effraction

effusive

eggcorn

egress

El Niño

embolus

embryo

emeritus

eminent

emissary

emulsify

en masse

ensconced

ensued

entente

environs

epenthesis

epicurean

epidermis

epidural

episcopal

epithet

epitome

epoch

equilibrium

equinox

equivalent

equivocate

eradicate

ermine ——●   noun – any of several weasels that have white fur in winter.

errata

erroneous

erstwhile

erubescent

eructation

escarpment

eschew

espousal

estuary

ethanol

étude

eucalyptus

eucrasia

euphonious

europium

eustress

Evactor

evacuees

evanescent

evo-devo

evzone

ewer

ex libris

exaugural

excelsior

excision

execrable

exeunt

exiguous

exodus

exogenous

exorbitant

expatiate

expectorant

expostulate

expugnable

expunge

exsect

extant

extemporaneous

extrapolate

extravasate

extrorse

F

facile

factitious

facundity

fajitas

farcical

fardel

farina

farkleberry

Farsi

farthingale

fatuously

fealty

feckless

fecund

feign

fenestrated

fenster

fervorous

festooned

feudalism

fiat

fibula

fictile

Ficus

fiduciary

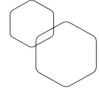

the first bee

In 1925, the first national spelling bee was organized by the Louisville Courier-Journal with a total of nine spellers. Frank Neuhauser won the championship title after correctly spelling "gladiolus."

finial
fipple
firkin
fjeld
flagellum
flagon
flambé
flaneur
flavedo
flèche
flittern
Florentine
floribunda
floruit
flotsam
FLOTUS
fluoride
focaccia
follicle
fontina
forbivorous
fortissimo
Franciscan
fratority
fraudulent
frazil —●   noun – ice crystals sometimes similar to slush that are formed in turbulent water.
freneticism
Freudian
frison
frittata
froufrou
froward
fructiferous
frugivore
fucoid
fugue
fulgent
fulminate
funambulist
fungible
furcula
fusiform
fussbudget

G

galapago

Gallic
galvanize
gambit
ganache
gasiform
gastronome
gaudery
gaur
gelatinous
Gemini
genealogical
geniture
genome
gentilitial
geocaching
geriatric
germane
gibbous
gingivitis
gladiatorial
glareous
glazier
glissando
globular
gluttonous
gnocchi
goji berry
golem
Goliath
goosander
gossamer
Gothamite
grande dame
grandiloquent
grandrelle
graticule
gratis —●   adverb – without charge : free.
gravimetry
gravitas
greaves
Gregorian
grissino
groats
grobian
grotesqueness
grouse

gubernatorial
gudgeon
gules
gullibility
gumption
gustatory

H

habeas corpus
habiliments
hackneyed
hagiographer
halibut
Halifax
hallucinate
haplography
harangue
harbinger
harrier
harrumph
Hathor
hauberk
hauteur
Hawaiian
hawok
heinousness
heleoplankton
heliacal
hennery
heptad —●   noun – a group of seven people or things.
hermeneutics
hermetically
herringbone
heterochromia
heterophony
hetman
heuristic
hibernaculum
hierurgical
hinoki
hipsterism
histrionics
Hitchcockian
hoity-toity
holmium
Holocaust

hologram
Holstein
homeostasis
homester
homiletics
hubris
humerus
humidistat
hummock
Hungary
hydrangea
hydrocortisone
hydrophobia
hydroponic
hypochondria
hypogeous
hypotenuse
hyrax

I
ibex
ibuprofen
Icarian
idiosyncratic
ignominious
illative
illicitly
illustrious
immolate
immortality
impasto
impeachable
impecunious
impediment
imperious
impermeable
impetus
implacable
implicative
impoverish
impresario
impromptu

incinerate
incisiform — ● adjective – having the form of a tooth adapted for cutting.
incitive
inclement
incoherent
incompetent
incubate
indemnity
indicia
indict
indigent
indistinguishable
indolent
inducement
indulgent
ineffable
ineluctable
ineptitude
inerrancy
ingenuous
ingratiate
inimical
injurious
inoculate
insignia
instigate
insufflator
interred
interrogative
intersperse
intuitable
inveterate
inviolable
iridescent
irrevocable
Isle Royale

J
jactance
jadeite
jalapeño
jambalaya

jarl
jaundiced
jeepney
jettison
jicama
jiggery-pokery
jimberjawed
jingoism
jitney
jocularity
jubilant — ● adjective – expressing gladness or triumphant joy.
judicious
julienne
Jurassic
justiciable
juvenilia
juxtapose

K
kaiser
kanban
kanji
karst
kerchief
kinesiology
kleptocrat
koto — ● noun – a long Japanese zither having 13 silk strings.
krausen
krypton
kufi
kugel
kung pao

L
labroid
labyrinthine
laceration
laconic
lacustrine
laity
lambasted
lambently

did you know?

The Scripps National Spelling Bee was featured in the 2002 Academy Award-nominated documentary *Spellbound*.

lambkin
languorous
lanolated
lantana
lapidary
larceny
largesses
larnax
lassitude
latigo
laudatory
laureate
lavender
legalese
legato
legerity
lemniscus
leviathan
liaise
lidocaine
limned
limousine
limpa
limpet
limpid
limpkin
lingua franca
linnet
linstock
lithium
lithophone
litmus
lobotomy
locavore ———● noun – a person who eats foods grown nearby whenever possible.
loch
logarithmic
logographic
lolled
longitude
lorikeet
lossy
lousicide
lovage
luculent
ludicrous
lugubrious
lumen

luthier
lutrine
luxuriate

M
machination
mackerel
macropterous
macular
malapropism
malevolent
malfeasance
malinger
mandrill
mano a mano
manumit
marimba
marionette
marring
marsupial
mastodon
matriculation
mawkish
McCoy
Mecca
medusa
megalomaniac
melamine
melee
melismatic
menagerie
mendacious
mendicity
meningitis
mephitic
merganser
meridian
merino
mesial
Mesopotamian
metaplasia
metastasize
metatarsal
MIDI
millennial
millet
millisecond

millivolt
minacious
minestra
minette
minuscule**
    OR miniscule
Miranda
misnomer
mitigative
mitochondria
mochi
modiste
moissanite
mollify
monitory
monochrome
monture
moratorium
mordant
Moroccan
morphological
mortician
Motrin
movimento
muchacha
mulligan
Munich
municipal
musketeers
Mylar
myocarditis
myoglobin
myopic ———● adjective – lacking in foresight or keenness of insight.

N
Namibian
nanotechnology
narcoleptic
nautilus
Neapolitan
necrotic
nectarine
neonatology
neoterism
nepotism
netiquette
neuropathy

neuroticism
Newfoundland
nexus
nitrate
nocive
noctambulist
no-goodnik
nomancy ——● noun – divination by letters.
nomenclature
nomophobia
nonage
nonchalance
nonnegotiable
nonvolatile
Norovirus
Nostradamus
notoriety
novemdecillion
noxious
nuance
nubuck
nuciform
nucleated
numerology
nutation
nutria
nuzzer

O
obfuscate
oblique
obloquy
obnebulate
obsecration
obsolete
obstetrician
obstreperous ——● adjective – stubborn and defiant often with a show of noisy disorder.
occipital
occultation
Oceanian
octonocular

octuplicate
odometer
officinal
okapi
olfactory
olingo
ombudsman
omnilegent
omniscient
onus
oompah
operose
opprobrious
oppugn
Orion
orthogonal
oscitation
osculatory
Osloite
osmosis
osprey
ossicle
ostensibly
osteopath
ottoman
oxalis

P
pagoda
palatable
Paleozoic
palpebral
palpitant
panary ——● adjective – related to breadmaking.
pancetta
pancreas
panegyric
pantomime
papyrus
par excellence
parabola

parameters
paraplegic
parasol
pariah
parliamentary
parochial
parodic
parr
parsimony
particulate
parturient
parvo
pashmina
Patagonia
patella
pathos
patronymic
paucity
peacenik
peculate
pecuniary
pedantry
pelagial
pelerine
pelf
pendragon
pendulous
penitentiary
pepita
per se
peradventure
perceptible
perilous
periodontist
peripheral
periwinkle
permutation
perpetrator
perquisite
perseverance
perspicacious

there's a first time for everything

Hugh Tosteson was the first winner from outside of the 50 U.S. states. He lived in Puerto Rico and won in 1975.

persuasible
pertinacity
pestilence
petroleum
phalanges
phenotype
philosophize
phishing
phlebotomy
phoenix
phonetician
phosphorescent
phraseology
phycology
phylum
Pierre
piety
pilaster
pilcrow
pileus
pilferer
pilosity
pilotage
pinnacle
pinnate
pious
pituitary
placoderm
plagiarism
plaintiff
planetesimal
plangency
planisphere
planogram
plantain
plantigrade
plaudits
plenipotentiary
plenitude
plentiful
Plumeria
plutonomy
poblano
podsnappery
Podunk
pointelle
politick

pollutant
polonium
poltroon
polyester
polygenous
polypeptide
polysemy
polysyllabic
pomato
pomegranate
Pomeranian
pomology
pompeii
pomposity
pongee
pontiff
populace
porcelain
porosity
portentous
portico
posada
posse
possessive
posterity
posthumous
postural
potassium
praxis
prehensile
prelapsarian
preponderance
preposterous
preprandial
presentient
prespinous
prevenient
prima donna
primeval**
    OR primaeval
primogeniture
princeps
privatim
privet
probative
procurement
prodigious

profligacy
profundity
proletarian
proliferate
prolix
prolusory
promontory
propinquity
proprietary
proprioceptive
prorogue
prosody
protectorate
protuberant
provenance
proviant
provincial
proviso
psychoanalysis
puchero
pugilist
pugnacious
pulchritude
purvey
pyrite
pyrotechnics

Q

quadriceps
quadrilateral
quadrillion
qualms
quid pro quo
quiddity ———● noun – the ultimate form or the essential nature of something.
quinary
quince
quintessential
quirt
quittance
quotidian
QWERTY

R

rabato
rabbinic
rambla
rambunctious

25

ramifications	repository	salience
ramson	reprieve	saltatory
rankles	reprisal	sapphire
rapscallion	Requiem	sardonic
raptatorial	requisition	sarmentum
rasorial	resilience	sartorial
raucous	resplendence	sashay
reagent	restitutory	saturnine
realgar	résumé	sauger
realm	resuscitate	scarab
Realtor	retinol	scarlatina
rebarbative	retinoscopy	scenographer
reboation	retrocedence	schism
recipient	retrodict	schnell
reciprocity	retrograde	schooner
reconcilable	revenant	scintillation
reconnoiter**	reverberant	sclerosis
OR reconnoitre	rhapsody	scrivener
recreant	rhizome	scrumptiously
recriminatory	rhythmically	scumble
recumbent	ricochet	scuppers
recusancy	rictus	scythe
redolent	rigatoni	secant
refrigerant	ritziness	secession
refugium	rollicking	sedentary
regalia	Romano	sedge
reggae	rosin	sedum
regicide	roustabout	seethe
regnal	Rubicon	senecio
regurgitate	rudiments	seneschal
reimbursable	rugose	senna
reminiscent	ruminate	sensei
remonstrance	rustication	septennial
remuda		sepulchral
remuneration	**S**	sequential
renegotiate	sabbatical	seraphic
renitency	sabermetrics	serrated
reparations	sabotage	sesame
repartee	sacrament	settee
repentant	sacrosanct	severance
repercussion	sailage	shaman

regurgitate — verb – to bring, forcefully impel, or pour back out again.

archaic or obsolete? not here.

The Bee doesn't include words labeled obsolete or archaic in competition lists, and you won't find any in *2024 Words of the Champions* either. Why? Because they're just not used that often. Words labeled obsolete are found in literature but have not been part of standard English since 1755; words labeled archaic are only used rarely or in special contexts such as prayers or poetry since 1755. Why 1755? That was the year that the first really large and comprehensive dictionary was published in London by Samuel Johnson.

shar-pei
shazam
shebang
sheldrake
shenanigans
Shetland
shirk
shoji
sieve
simpatico
simultaneity
singultus
sirenian
Sirius
slalom
slumgullion
smellfungus   noun – someone who tends to find fault in others.
smithereens
snell
sobersides
sobriety
solon
somatotype
somniloquy
soothsayer
sophomoric
soppiness
sousaphone
Spaniel
spathe
speciation
spectrometer
spinosity
spiracle
spirulina
splenetic
sponsalia
spontaneity
sprightliness
sprue
spurious
stagflation
staid
stalwart
stanchion
statistician
statuesque

statusy
stegosaur
steinkirk
   OR steenkirk
stellular
steppe
stevia
stigmata
stimuli
stipulate
stratification
stratocracy
stratosphere
striation
stricture
stridency
Styrofoam
subliminal
subluxated
submersible
subrident
subsequent
subsistence
subterranean
subtlety
subversive
succumb
succussion
suet
suffrage
Sumatran
summoned
superficiality
superstitious
supine
supplicate
supremacy
surcease
surety
surmountable
surrealist
suture
sycophant
syllabus
sylph
symmetrical
symposium

syndicate
syntonize
syntrophism
syringe

T

tabernacle
tableau
tabulate
taciturn
tae kwon do
tai chi
talisman
tamworth
tangerine
tantrum
tapioca
tappet
tarantula
tarlatan**
   OR tarleton
Tasmanian
taverna
taxonomic
tectonic
teemed
telepathic
telmatology
temblor
temerity
tempestuous
tempura
tenaciously
tenement
tensile
tentacled
tepidity
tercentenary
terminus
terra-cotta
terrarium
tetanus
Thailand
theomachy
theorem
theosophy
theriatrics

thoracic
thoroughbred
thrasonical
thwartwise
thyme
tibia
tiffany
tiffin
Tinseltown
titian
titration
tomfoolery
tommyrot —● noun – complete foolishness or nonsense.
tomography
tongue
toorie
topgallant
topiary
toploftical
toponymic
torsion
tortoise
tosh
toties quoties
toxicosis
tractability
traiteur
transcend
transducer
transhumance
transience
transmissibility
transmontane
transpiration
transposable
trapezoid
travails
treadle
trefoil
trellis
tremulous

trepanation
trepidation
triage
tributary
trice
tricenary
triceratops
triforium
trigeminal
triglycerides
trillium
triste
trituration
trophic
Truckee
truncheon
tsk-tsked
tubular
tumpline
tungsten
turbinado
turducken
turgor
turken
turophile
turpentine
tussock
tutelage
tutti-frutti
twain
twang
tympanum
typhlology

U
ufology
Ukrainian
ulna —● noun – the inner of the two bones of the forearm.
umbilical
umbrage
una corda

unchristened
unctuous
ungetatable
unilaterally
univocal
unmoored
unremitting
unscathed
untenable
upbraid
upsilon
ursine
usurper
utilitarian
uveal
uvula

V
vaccination
vacillate
vagabonds
vague
vainglorious
valedictorian
valerian
valiant
valuator
vandalize
vanguard
vanquish
vantage
varicose
variegated
Vatican
vaudeville
veganism
vegetarian
vehemence
vehicular
vendage
veneer

older than sliced bread
The first national spelling bee was held in 1925. That makes us older than sliced bread, bubble gum and even trampolines.

venerable

vengeance

venial

venomous

ventail

ventricle

ventriloquy

veracity

verbena

verism

veritable

vermicide

vernal

vertigo

vespertine

vestibule

vetiver

vetoed

vicarious

vice versa

vicenary

viceroy

victimology

vigil

vincible

virga

virulence

vis-à-vis

viscidity

vitriolic

volary

   OR volery

volatile

volition

volucrine

volumetric

Vulcan ——————● noun – a worker in metals; especially: a blacksmith.

W

wallaby

Walter Mitty

widdershins ——————● adverb – counterclockwise.

wilco

wobbulator

woebegone

wolfsbane

wootz

Y

yabbies ——————● plural noun – small burrowing crayfish that live in most Australian creeks and water holes.

yardang

yawmeter

Yorkshire

Z

zazen

zeitgeist

zeppelin

zirconium

zocalo

zoetic

zoolatry

zowie

zurna ——————● noun – a traditional Middle Eastern woodwind instrument.

zydeco

zygote

The Bee's Bookshelf

The Bee's Bookshelf is the official online book club of the Scripps National Spelling Bee. It's a place to explore the connection between stories and spelling. Each month, we read a new book together and share insights, so sign up to receive our monthly emails to find out which book is next. Visit spellingbee.com/book-club to learn more.

school spelling bee study list

The seventh and eighth-grade words from the 2024 School Spelling Bee Study List. Words with a single asterisk (*) indicate a primarily British spelling. Words with a double asterisk (**) are the preferred spelling.

tripe	incarnated	ellipsis
slakes	pews	thyroid
Illinois	malicious	elongated
commandments	interstellar	lasso**
contagion	petticoat	OR lassoo
decibels	insufferable	incandescent
repose	spawned	bureaucrats
nondescript	gorilla	refuge
expulsion	quarry	shoal
Laundromat	kung fu	perpendicularity
pervading	steeds	antechamber
malnutrition	destitution	jeopardy
tunic	patronize	sauna
extravagant	OR patronise*	conciliatory
innards	dilute	forsook
acclimate	societal	boba
recede	uncanny	animatronics
indignant	communing	frijoles
wok	deadpan	minimus
categorically	arable	senescent
demure	surfactant	secreted
chasm	nitrogen	aspirin
hitherto	paralysis	aptitude
horticulture	metronome	Chicana
magistrates	attorney	bilge
sprocket	snivel	simultaneously
punctually	contemptible	Copenhagen
dynasty	altimeter	Bunsen burner
koi	jugular	defoliant
incense	insolent	aerosol
incited	aura	Ramadan**
deficiencies	propitious	OR Ramadhan

repose — noun – a state of resting after activity or strain.

find the bee on social media

Connect with us! If you're 13 or older, follow the Scripps National Spelling Bee on social media. You can find us on Instagram, Facebook and Twitter. Use #spellingbee to join the conversation.

photosynthesis

malignant

matterhorn

divot

pixels

antonyms

Trinidadian

mangels

nopales

Gilgamesh — noun – a legendary Sumerian king and hero of a particular long narrative poem.

conjunto

Sumerian

pinyin

Taoism**

   OR Daoism

lymphoma

scandium

dendrochronology

palomino**

   OR palamino

retinitis pigmentosa

fens

haw

peplos**

   OR peplus

moira

Erlenmeyer flask

Samian

luciferin

megaron

sphagnum

pronaos

craquelure

Macao

   OR Macau

silicon

Albuquerque

Mumbai

turquoise**

   OR turquois

Assam

lanthanides

antimony

amphoras — plural noun – ancient Greek jars or vases having large oval bodies, narrow cylindrical necks, and two handles.

hypocaust

avens

grebe

pipette**

   OR pipet

leks

pullets

Macedonia

centrifuge

coleus

Tetrazzini

Pleiades

coccidiosis

rooibos tea

Versailles

meitnerium

Okefenokee

Popocatepetl

Shaanxi

our namesake

Although the first national spelling bee occurred in 1925, it wasn't until 1941 that Scripps-Howard Newspapers, now known as The E.W. Scripps Company, assumed leadership of the program.

difficulty level: three bee
Words of the Champions

Organized alphabetically, these words are a great place to complete your journey of mastering *Words of the Champions*! Words with a single asterisk (*) indicate a primarily British spelling. Words with a double asterisk (**) are the preferred spelling. A complete list of the words that were added to this year's study list can be found on page 40.

A

à fond
à la grecque
a posteriori
ab aeterno
abaculus
abraum
acacia
accordatura
acerola
acetaminophen
acetone
acharya
Achernar
acicula
acidophilus
acoel
acrogeria
acropachy
ad nauseam
adiabatic
adieu
adscititious
Aegilops
aegrotat
aerophilatelic
aes rude
Aesir
affiche
ageusia
agitprop
Aglaia
agrypnia

ague
ahimsa
ahuatle
Ahuehuete
Ahura Mazda
ailette
aistopod
Aitutakian
ajimez
akaryote
akkum
alate
alcarraza
Alfvén
alleluiatic
allochroous
almuerzo
alouatte
alpargata
altazimuth
amaryllis
amour propre
amphistylar
amuse-gueule
anabathmoi
anaphylaxis
anathema
ancien régime
andouille
anemone
angiitis
aniseikonia
Anno Hegirae

anomaliped
anosognosia
antenatus
Antigua
Apabhramsa
ape-ape
aperçu
aphasia
Apistogramma
apocryphal
apophyge
Apostolici
Appaloosa
appetitost
après
Aramaic
Ardhamagadhi
Ardipithecus
ardoise
arenaceous
aretalogy
as nas
ascites
astaxanthin
Asura
asylee
attacca
au bleu
au courant
au jus
avgolemono — ● noun – a chicken soup made with egg yolks and lemon juice.
azotea
azulejo

home sweet home
While many people think the Bee is headquartered in Washington, D.C., our hive is actually located in Cincinnati, Ohio.

B

baccate
bagwyn
bahr
bahuvrihi
bailiwick
balata
balbriggan
baleen
banh mi
Barnumesque
Bartókian
Barylambda
bas-relief
batamote
battue
Baucis
bauxite
bavardage
Beauceron
beaumontage
Beaux arts
beccafico
Bêche-de-Mer
becquerel
ben trovato
Beowulf
berceuse
bergère
Bernoulli effect
bêtise
betony
beurre
Bezier curve
bhangra
bhikshuni
bibelot
bibimbap
bisbigliando
bismillah
blatherskite
blottesque

bobolink ●━━ noun – a small American songbird that resembles the blackbird.
Boise
Bolognese
boniface
bordereaux
Bosc
bouclé
boudin
bouillon
boulevardier
boutade
boutonniere
bozzetto
Braeburn
brouhaha
brume
bruschetta
buccal
buñuelo
Bunyanesque
Burkinabe

C

cabochon
ca'canny
cacaxte
cachexia
cacoëthes
Caerphilly
cahiers
caique
cairn
caisson
calabash
calamondin
calligram
caló
calusar
calvities
camarilla
Camembert
canaille

cantatrice
caprifig
Caracas
carcajou
carrageenan**
   OR carrageenin
   OR carragheenin
Carrickmacross
cartouches
caryatid
Casimir effect
Castalia
catachresis
cataphora
catarrh
catjang
cavalletti
caveola
cephalopod
cermet
chalaza
Chalcolithic
champignon
Charon
chastushka
chasuble
cheongsam
chèvre
chicanery
chopine
chorten
choucroute
ciénaga**
   OR cienega
ciliopathy
cioppino
cire perdue
cirri
clerihew
cobalamin
coccygeal
colcannon

on a global scale
At just 12 years old, Jody-Anne Maxwell from Kingston, Jamaica was our first international champion. She won the Bee in 1998.

colloque
colporteur**
   OR colporter
colubrine
concatenate
connoisseur
consanguine
consigliere
consommé
contrapposto
contretemps
copernicium
corrigenda
corybantic
coterie
cotoneaster
coulibiac
coulisse
coulrophobia
coup de grace
courgette
couverture
creances —● plural noun – fine lines used to leash a hawk during training.
crokinole
croquembouche
croquignole
croustade
cryptozoa
cushag
cynocephali

D
daguerreotype
Darjeeling
darmstadtium
de rigueur
decastich
degauss
Deimos
Delmarva Peninsula
demitasse
démodé
demurrage
Déné
dengue
dentifrice
derring-do

Deseret
desiccate
Devanagari
dghaisa
dhole
dhurrie
diapason
diaphanous
diastole
Djibouti
dragée
drahthaar
Dubhe
Dubuque
duello
duxelles
dvandva
Dvorak —● noun – a typing keyboard with frequently used letters placed centrally.
dysphasia
dysrhythmia

E
ecchymosis
echelon
echinoderm
edamame
effete
effleurage
Egeria
eisteddfod —● noun – a Welsh competitive festival of the arts especially in singing.
élan
eleemosynary
eluate
embouchure
emollient
emolument
emphysema
ennui
Enoch Arden
enoki
epideictic
epistemology
epixylous
Equatoguinean
Erewhonian
Eris
erythroblast

Esau
escarole
escheator
esclandre
escritoire
espadrille
espalier
espial
esplanade
estancia
estovers
estrepe
ethylene
étouffée
eudiometer
Euroclydon
exchequer

F
farfalle
farouche
farrago
fatshedera
fauchard
Feldenkrais
fellahin**
   OR fellaheen
fêng shui
ferruginous
fête champêtre
fetticus
fibromyalgia
Firbolg —● plural noun – an ancient group of people in Ireland.
flehmen
force majeure
Formica
foudroyant
frabjous
fracas
funori
furan
Furneaux
furuncle

G
gabarit
gabbro

gaffe

   OR gaff

gagaku

Gaia

gaillardia

Galahad

galatea

galena

gallivat

galoot

gambol

Gaspesian

gasthaus

gattine

Geatish

gegenschein

gendarme

genet

gesellschaft

giallolino ———● noun – any of a variety of yellow pigments.

ginglymus

Gippsland

glabella

glacis

glengarry

glyceraldehyde

goanna

Gondwana

graywacke

griot

Groenendael

Gruyère

guan

guapena

Guarnerius

guayabera

guerite

guichet

Guidonian

Gurmukhi

gyascutus

gyokuro

gypsophila

gypsum

H

halala

   OR halalah

halcyon

Hamtramck

hangul

haupia

hebdomadal

Hebrides

hei-tiki

hellebore

hemorrhage

henotheism

hepatectomy

Herodotean

hiortdahlite

Hippolyta

hirsute

hoi polloi ———● plural noun – ordinary people : multitude, masses.

holobenthic

hominin

homoscedasticity

hordeolum

hsaing-waing

Hsia

Huallaga

huerta

Humboldt

hutia**

   OR jutia

hypaethral

hyssop

hysteresis

hysteron proteron

I

ichthyology

icosahedron

ikat

ikebana

immie

in medias res

in silico

incunabula

inglenook

ingot

insouciance

integument

internecine

interregnum

Inugsuk

Inuk ———● noun – a member of the Inuit people.

isagoge

Ishihara test

isosceles

ivermectin

J

jai alai

jalousie

janthina

jasmone

je ne sais quoi

jerboa

joropo

Jumada ———● noun – either of two months of the Islamic year.

Jungian

K

kakapo

kaleidoscope

kalimba

kalopanax

Kannada

kapparah

katakana

katana

kathakali

the history of silent letters

What's up with all those silent letters?! The word "debt," for example, comes from a Latin word *debita*, which comes from *debitum*, meaning "debt." French borrowed the word and dropped the "b," but a few hundred years after the word passed to English, we put the "b" back in to make it closer to the original Latin. Why? Probably just to make it look more "classical," but it sure does make it harder to spell!

kepi
Keplerian
kerril ———• noun – an Asiatic sea snake.
Keynesian
kichel
kipuka
Kitksan
kiva
Kjeldahl
kobold
koh-i-noor
Koine
koji
korrigan
krewe
kriegspiel
Kuiper Belt
kwashiorkor
kyphoplasty

L
La Tène
laccolith
lanceolate
langrage
laterigrade
Latinxua
lebensraum
leberwurst ———• noun – liver sausage.
lebkuchen
lecithin
lefse
lierre
ligas
lilliputian
limaçon
Llullaillaco
lobscouse
loess**
   OR löss
logothete
lokelani
louche
loupe
luftmensch
lunulae

M
macaque
macchiato
macigno
mackinaw
macushla
mademoiselle
maillot
majuscule
Makgadikgadi Pans
malaise
Mandelbrot set
mandorla
mandragora
mange-tout
mangonel
Manu
maquillage
Marathi
marcel
marcescent
maringouin
martinoe
mascarpone
mässig
mediobrome
medulla
megacephalic
megrims
meiosis
mele
mellifluous
Menaia
meringue
Metonic cycle
microfiche
millegrain
Mirach
miscible
mittimus
moiety
mondegreen
MOOC
moraine ———• noun – a collection of earth and stones carried and finally deposited by a glacier.
moribund
morion

mortadella
motherumbung
mozo
muesli
mufti
muktuk
muliebrity
Muzak
myeloma

N
Nabal
nacelle
nahcolite
naïveté
naricorn
Naugahyde
naumachia
neem
neophyte
Ner Tamid
nescience
Nethinim
Nicoise
nictitate
nidicolous
nimiety
niminy-piminy ———• adjective – absurdly nice: ridiculously delicate: finicky.
nisi
nival
ni-Vanuatu
niveau
nodosity
nonpareil
notturno
noumenon
nouveau
Novanglian
nudibranch
nyctinasty

O
obeisant
odontiasis
oeuvre
ogival

olecranon
oleiculture
onomatopoeia
onychorrhexis
oolite
oopuhue
Oort cloud
oppidan
Orinoco
ormolu ● noun – brass made to imitate gold and used for furniture and other decorative purposes.
orogeny
orphéon
oryx
ostium
otiose
Ouagadougou
oud
outré
oviparous
oxyacetylene

P

pachyderm
paella
pahoehoe
palaver
palooka
pampootie
panacea
Panathenaea
Panchen Lama
panettone
panjandrum
pannose
papillon
pappardelle
parallax
paramahamsa
pareidolia
Parmentier
parquet

parterre
pas seul
pasilla
pastitsio
patois
Patripassianism
pejorate
pekoe
Pepysian
perciatelli
perianth
petechia
Philistine
philopatry
phloem
phlox
Phobos
photovoltaic
piatti
piccata
pierrot
piloncillo
pinniped
piscivorous
pistou
Plantagenet
pneumatocyst
pochoir
podagra
point d'appui
Ponzi
portmanteau
portugais
porwigle ●  noun – a tadpole.
pot-au-feu
pothos
potpourri
pou sto
poudre B
prajna
pralltriller

pratique
prêt-à-porter
prion
Promethean
promyshlennik
pruritus
psalmody
pschent
psoriasis
ptyxis
pudibund
puerilely
pylorus
Pythagorean
Pyxis

Q

qiyas
Quaoar
quasar
quattrocento
Quito
quokka ● noun – a small, stocky wallaby with a reddish-brown coat and a short tail.
quonk
Quonset

R

raclette
rafflesia
rajpramukh
ranunculus
rapparee
rapprochement
Rastafarian
Rayleigh wave
realpolitik
recamier
redingote ● noun – a lightweight woman's coat that is belted with the front open.
rembrandt
rennet
renvoi

it's all Greek to me

We often get questions about why we use words that may not appear to be English. Most words in the English language are words that we borrowed from other languages. We borrowed them, used them and now call them our own.

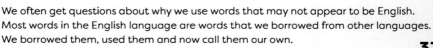

rescissible

revanche

reveille

rhododendron

rhyton

rinceau

risorgimento

risposta

rissole

Robigalia

rocaille

roi fainéant

rond de jambe

rondeau

ronin

rooseveltite

rosemaling

roseola

rouille

rubaiyat

rubato

rubefacient

ruelle

runcible spoon

rupicolous

ruscus

rutabaga

ryas

Ryeland

Ryukyu

S

saccharide

saeta

Sagittarius

sakura

salmagundi**

OR salmagundy

sambal

samsara

Sangamon

sangfroid

sannyasi

Saoshyant

Sapporo

savoir faire

Sbrinz

scaberulous

scagliola

Schedar

schefflera

sciatica

sciolistic

sclaff

scobiform

scrofula

scurrilous

seine

selah

semaphore

seraya

serin

sesquipedalian

sessile

seton

Sfax

sforzando

Shawwal

Shiba Inu

shubunkin

silique

Sir Roger de Coverley

Skeltonic

skerrick

smriti**

OR smrti

soirée

sororal

sorrel

sostenuto

souchong

sous vide

spiedini

spodumene

sprechstimme

sravaka

stevedore

Strelitzia

stretto

Strigolniki

stroganoff

struthious

stupa

sturnine

stygian

styptic

succès fou

succorance

OR succourance*

Sufi

supercilious

surimi

surreptitious

svarabhakti —● noun – the introduction of a vowel sound in Sanskrit especially between r or l and a following consonant.

Svengali

sybaritic

synanthrope

syncope

T

taal

tachycardia

tachyon

taedium vitae

tamarack

tamari

tambour

tam-o'-shanter

tanager

tandoori

tannined

taoiseach

tapetum

tardigrade

tarpaulin

taurine

Tchefuncte

Tegucigalpa

telamon

teledu

telegnosis

temalacatl

tempeh

teneramente

terai

teraphim

teratism

terra nullius

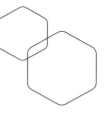

Terre Haute

tessitura

tetrachoric

Teutonic

thalassic

theca

Theravada

thimerosal

Thomism

thuluth

tic douloureux

tikka

tikkun

tilleul

tinamou

tinnient

tintinnabulary

tiramisu

tmesis

toccata

toey

toile

Tok Pisin

tokonoma

tomahawk

tomalley

tonsillitis

topazolite

toque

toreutics

torii

toril

tourelle

tournedos

towhee

trichinosis

triduum

trillado

triquetra

triskelion

tristeza

trochee

trompe l'oeil

trous-de-loup

trouvaille

tryptophan

tsukupin

tullibee ●

turmeric

tusche

Typhoean

noun – a whitefish of central and northern North America.

U

ubi sunt

ubiquinone

ullage

ululate

unakite ——●

unguiculate

uraeus

urushiol

ushabti

Ushuaia

usufruct

noun – an opaque igneous rock flecked with green, black, pink, and white that is used as a gemstone.

V

varicella

velouté

verisimilitude

vermeil

Véronique

vexillologist ——●

viaticum

vicissitudes

vigneron

vignette

vilipend

villi

vinaceous

vinaigrette

vitiate

vituperative

vizierial

noun – a specialist in the study of flags.

W

wabeno

Waf

wahine

Wampanoag

wapiti

wassail

weka

weltschmerz

Wensleydale ——●

wentletrap

whippoorwill

whydah**

   OR whidah

wigan

wildebeest

witch of Agnesi

wushu

noun – a white cheese that is eaten fresh prior to preserving.

X

xerogel

xiphias

xyloglyphy ●

noun – wood sculpting that is artistic in nature.

Y

yakitori

yosenabe ——●

yttriferous

yuga

yuloh

yuzu

noun – a soup made of vegetables and seafood in broth.

Z

zacate

zaibatsu

Zamboni

Zanni

zapateado

Zdarsky tent

zemi

zimocca

zortzico

zugzwang ●

noun – the need to make a move in chess when it is not to one's advantage.

did you know?

The Scripps National Spelling Bee has declared co-champions in 1950, 1957, 1962, 2014, 2015, 2016 and 2019. In fact, in 2019 we had octo-champs!

Words that are new this year!

With each edition of *Words of the Champions*, 20% of the words are replaced with brand new words! This includes each year's new School Spelling Bee Study List, but it also includes words at the One, Two and Three Bee levels of *Words of the Champions*. Below is the complete list of this year's newly added words that are not also on the School Spelling Bee Study List. Words with a single asterisk (*) indicate a primarily British spelling. Words with a double asterisk (**) are the preferred spelling.

Please note: These words are included in the full list in the previous pages. We've compiled them here for you for ease of studying.

A
abashed
abject
ablation
aboriginal
abraum
acclaim
acidophilus
acupuncture
addendum
addition
admonition
adnate
advection
affiche
affiliate
agility
agrypnia
alienate
alimentation
analects
anionic
anise
anklet
anneal
anniversary
anomaliped
anosognosia
ape-ape
appetitost
arrearage
Asiago
astronaut
asylee

atrabilious
attrition

B
baccate
bagwyn
become
billingsgate
birdie
bisbigliando
boarders
boffin
Boise
boogie-woogie
Braeburn
breathtaking
Broccolini
broil
bumblebee
busby

C
caducity
caique
calamondin
calcify
calvities
cancion
candid
cardoon
carrageenan**
    OR carrageenin
    OR carragheenin
cathode

catnap
caudex
cello
chamberlain
ciénaga**
    OR cienega
cloture
coach
cogitation
comminatory
commiserative
compelling
concision
confabulation
conglutinant
consideration
convention
copperhead
Coptic
corm
coroner
cynicism

D
daisy
decimation
declination
decurion delectable
Delmarva Peninsula
dghaisa diathermy
diatonic

40

dihedral
dimorphism
disaster
disjunct
diversion
drahthaar
dribbles
dromic
druid
drumlin
dysgraphia

E
eagerly
earmark
editorial
eisteddfod
ellipse
endearing
ensued
epistemology
epixylous
eructation
eucrasia
europium
evzone
excelsior
exeunt
explode
extradition
extraordinaire
extrorse

F
facundity
fadeaway
fardel
farthingale
feeble
fenster

fiat
fictile
finial
fipple
flight
flittern
flummery
folate
folly
foozle
foppery
forbivorous
fribble
fundamental
fusiform
fussbudget

G
gaffer
gaggle
galley
Gallic
gardenesque
gargle
genet
geniture
gizzard
Gondwana
grapple
gravimetry
gravitas
guapena

H
habitual
Hamtramck
hatchet
hennery
henotheism
Hitchcockian

hoagies
holmium
horseradish
howler
hypaethral
hysteresis

I
immortality
incisiform
incitive
income
incubate
indistinguishable
influential
insufflator
Inugsuk

J
jammer
jaundiced
jerboa

K
kazoo
kenning
koji
kriegspiel

L
labroid
laccolith
lambently
langrage
larnax
latigo
limelight
limned
limpet
limpkin

one dictionary to rule them all

linstock
lunulae
lutrine

M

macigno
madrigal
Makgadikgadi Pans
marring
metaplasia
Michigander
millet
millisecond
minestra
minette
mockery
modality
modem
modify
monture
morion
muliebrity
musings
myocarditis

N

naricorn
Norovirus
nozzles
nuzzer

O

obsecration
oopuhue
operose
Orinoco
oscitation
ostium
overtures

P

paginate
palooka

pannose
paraplegic
passage
pastime
perciatelli
perianth
periodontist
photovoltaic
piatti
pinnate
plantigrade
plentiful
podsnappery
polygenous
prajna
pralltriller
pratique
prelapsarian
preprandial
primogeniture
proliferate
prolusory
promyshlennik
prosody
proviant
proxy
ptyxis
purvey

Q

quirt
Quito

R

rankles
rapparee
rapscallion
rasorial
reagent
recanted
reconsider
recovery
refugium

remuda
renegotiate
renewable
renitency
rigatoni
rosemaling
ruscus

S

sannyasi
sarmentum
scandal
schnell
sci-fi
scobiform
sedum
seller
senna
sensei
sensory
September
shaggy
sloop
snell
solidity
solon
solvency
sorbet
speciation
sponsalia
sprechstimme
stance
steampunk
steinkirk
    OR steenkirk
stowaway
stratocracy
Styrofoam
subluxated
subsistence
subversive
succorance
    OR succourance*

suffix
Sufi
sybaritic
syntonize
syntrophism

T
tamworth
telmatology
tendency
terra nullius
theosophy
thrift
tikka
tilleul
titration
toastmaster
traiteur
transducer
transpiration
treadle
treasury
triage

trinkets
trophic
tubers
tumpline
tunnel
turducken
tutorial
twain
twang
typhlology

U
uppercut
usufruct

V
valerian
veneer
ventail
viceroy
vigil
vinaceous
viscidity

W
Wampanoag
wealthy
whydah**
    OR whidah
wimple

Y
yawl
yawmeter
yore

Z
zapateado
Zoetic

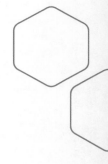

Word Club

Want a new way to study? The Word Club app, available for free in the App Store and the Google Play Store, will make mastering *Words of the Champions* fun! Choose from multiple different quiz and study options for both spelling and vocabulary, all with expert audio pronunciations from the Bee's head pronouncer, Dr. Jacques Bailly.

vocabulary: one bee, a-z

New this year, we've selected 26 of our favorite words from the One Bee section of *Words of Champions* (one for each letter of the alphabet) and included their definitions throughout this study guide. Below, you can find all of those definitions in one helpful place.

Want more vocabulary? Download the FREE Word Club app today to find definitions like these for all 4,000 *Words of the Champions* words.

alpaca – *noun* – a South American mammal that resembles a llama.

botany – *noun* – the science of plants.

conch – *noun* – an edible marine mollusk with a large spiral shell.

domino – *noun* – a small dotted slab that together with other such slabs is used to play a game.

elusive – *adjective* – hard to catch.

flipperling – *noun* – a small animal with broad flat limbs adapted for swimming (as a baby seal).

giggle – *verb* – to laugh in a silly manner.

husk – *noun* – one of the leaves enveloping an ear of corn.

ignite – *verb* – to set on fire.

jersey – *noun* – a soft knitted fabric used for making clothing, especially sportswear.

kudos – *noun* – praise given for some achievement.

limelight – *noun* – the center of public attention.

maritime – *adjective* – of or relating to navigation or commerce on the sea.

nuggets – *plural noun* – small usually round-shaped pieces of food.

oblong – *adjective* – having a shape that is elongated beyond a square or circle.

partridge – *noun* – a medium-sized, short-winged game bird with short legs and neck.

quirky – *adjective* – full of peculiarities.

restive – *adjective* – marked by fidgety or uneasy behavior.

salivate – *verb* – to produce an excessive amount of drool.

trumpet – *noun* – a brass instrument with a flared bell and three buttons pressed to make different notes.

usher – *noun* – someone who escorts people to seats at a gathering.

vicinity – *noun* – neighborhood.

windbaggery – *noun* – pompous meaningless talk.

yammer – *verb* – to talk rapidly, for a long time, and often loudly.

zither – *noun* – an instrument that has a shallow horizontal soundboard topped with 30 to 40 strings that are typically plucked by a performer.

piecing it together

A root can be a simple stand-alone word all by itself (like Greek *para* meaning "alongside") or a root can also be a word's core piece having a clearly identifiable meaning that, with the help of a suffix or prefix, makes a stand-alone word. Think about Dev Shah's 2023 winning word: "psammophile". The first part of this word contains the Greek root *psamm-* meaning "sand." The second part of Dev's word contains the Greek root *-phil* from the Greek word philos meaning "beloved, dear, loving." Put that together and… can you guess what the word means?

vocabulary: two bee, a-z

New this year, we've selected 26 of our favorite words from the Two Bee section of *Words of Champions* (one for each letter of the alphabet) and included their definitions throughout this study guide. Below, you can find all of those definitions in one helpful place.

aioli – *noun* – garlic mayonnaise.

bouffant – *adjective* – voluminous.

cantankerous – *adjective* – grumpy and argumentative.

dromic – *adjective* – of, relating to, or in the form of a racecourse.

ermine – *noun* – any of several weasels that have white fur in winter.

frazil – *noun* – ice crystals sometimes similar to slush that are formed in turbulent water.

gratis – *adverb* – without charge : free.

heptad – *noun* – a group of seven people or things.

incisiform – *adjective* – having the form of a tooth adapted for cutting.

jubilant – *adjective* – expressing gladness or triumphant joy.

koto – *noun* – a long Japanese zither having 13 silk strings.

locavore – *noun* – a person who eats foods grown nearby whenever possible.

myopic – *adjective* – lacking in foresight or keenness of insight.

nomancy – *noun* – divination by letters.

obstreperous – *adjective* – stubborn and defiant often with a show of noisy disorder.

panary – *adjective* – related to breadmaking.

quiddity – *noun* – the ultimate form or the essential nature of something.

regurgitate – *verb* – to bring, forcefully impel, or pour back out again.

smellfungus – *noun* – someone who tends to find fault in others.

tommyrot – *noun* – complete foolishness or nonsense.

ulna – *noun* – the inner of the two bones of the forearm.

Vulcan – *noun* – a worker in metals; especially: a blacksmith.

widdershins – *adverb* – counterclockwise.

yabbies – *plural noun* – small burrowing crayfish that live in most Australian creeks and water holes.

zurna – *noun* – a traditional Middle Eastern woodwind instrument.

all about the schwa

Be like a schwa – never stressed! Except that when you're a speller, a schwa can really stress you out! Why? A schwa is pronounced "uh" and in spelling can be any vowel: a, e, i, o, u or y. That can make a word pretty tough to spell. If you ask for the word's language of origin, you can try using that to help you out. If your word is from Greek, you might want to try an 'o' for that schwa, like in "bacteriolytic"!

vocabulary: three bee, a-z

New this year, we've selected 26 of our favorite words from the Three Bee section of *Words of Champions* (one for each letter of the alphabet) and included their definitions throughout this study guide. Below, you can find all of those definitions in one helpful place.

avgolemono – *noun* – a chicken soup made with egg yolks and lemon juice.

bobolink – *noun* – a small American songbird that resembles the blackbird.

creances – *plural noun* – fine lines used to leash a hawk during training.

Dvorak – *noun* – a typing keyboard with frequently used letters placed centrally.

eisteddfod – *noun* – a Welsh competitive festival of the arts especially in singing.

Firbolg – *plural noun* – an ancient group of people in Ireland.

giallolino – *noun* – any of a variety of yellow pigments.

hoi polloi – *plural noun* – ordinary people : multitude, masses.

Inuk – *noun* – a member of the Inuit people.

Jumada – *noun* – either of two months of the Islamic year.

kerril – *noun* – an Asiatic sea snake.

leberwurst – *noun* – liver sausage.

moraine – *noun* – a collection of earth and stones carried and finally deposited by a glacier.

niminy-piminy – *adjective* – absurdly nice : ridiculously delicate : finicky.

ormolu – *noun* – brass made to imitate gold and used for furniture and other decorative purposes.

porwigle – *noun* – a tadpole.

quokka – *noun* – a small, stocky wallaby with a reddish-brown coat and a short tail.

redingote – *noun* – a lightweight woman's coat that is belted with the front open.

svarabhakti – *noun* – the introduction of a vowel sound in Sanskrit especially between r or l and a following consonant.

tullibee – *noun* – a whitefish of central and northern North America.

unakite – *noun* – an opaque igneous rock flecked with green, black, pink, and white that is used as a gemstone.

vexillologist – *noun* – a specialist in the study of flags.

Wensleydale – *noun* – a white cheese that is eaten fresh prior to preserving.

xyloglyphy – *noun* – wood sculpting that is artistic in nature.

yosenabe – *noun* – a soup made of vegetables and seafood in broth.

zugzwang – *noun* – the need to make a move in chess when it is not to one's advantage.

consonants 101

Not sure whether the word has one consonant or two? Check to see if the word has a suffix, such as a verb that has been conjugated. These words often – but not always! – have a doubled consonant before that suffix. "The speckled frog *hopped* off the log while the horse *plodded* down the lane and the train *chugged* down the tracks." In each of these cases, the vowel before the doubled letter is a short sound. Can you spot others like this, and some that have long vowel sounds and do not double that consonant?

themed lists, games and puzzles

New this year, we hope the activities and lists below will provide you with a more engaging way to interact with and study the *Words of the Champions*. All of the words in the lists and games that follow appear in this year's edition of *Words of the Champions*. Enjoy!

themed lists

ologies

Ology means "a branch of knowledge" or "the study of."
Check out these words that all end in -ology. What do
you think they mean?

1. phycology
2. phraseology
3. nanotechnology
4. anthropology
5. numerology
6. neonatology
7. campanology
8. ufology
9. victimology
10. ichthyology
11. kinesiology
12. cetology
13. pomology

foods

You better make yourself a snack while you're
studying this list of food-related words!

1. chowder
2. crumpet
3. hazelnut
4. paella
5. rutabaga
6. frittata
7. jalapeño
8. jambalaya
9. tapioca
10. edamame
11. tiramisu
12. gnocchi
13. stroganoff
14. ganache

themed lists

animals

Lions and tigers and...alpacas, oh my! Check out this list of animals found in *Words of the Champions*.

1.	flounder	11.	crocodile
2.	ewe	12.	mandrill
3.	caterpillar	13.	labradoodle
4.	bonobo	14.	okapi
5.	tortoise	15.	aardvark
6.	mackerel	16.	ibex
7.	alpaca	17.	wallaby
8.	macaw	18.	tarantula
9.	cicada	19.	Shar-Pei
10.	lorikeet	20.	jerboa

music

Did you know that many of the spellers at the National Competition are also accomplished musicians? Learning these musical words can help you on your path to becoming a spelling bee superstar too!

1.	harmonious	8.	orchestra
2.	trumpet	9.	marimba
3.	con forza	10.	serenade
4.	mambo	11.	glissando
5.	cantor	12.	acoustic
6.	sousaphone	13.	muzak
7.	cadence	14.	accordatura

words that make you giggle

We know that spelling can be a serious business, but it's also really fun! Could you keep a straight face if you got one of these words at the microphone?

1. dillydally
2. whirlybird
3. riffraff
4. munchkin
5. bilbo
6. tutti-frutti
7. festooned
8. fisticuffs
9. burgoo
10. sashay

11. bandicoot
12. froufrou
13. gibbous
14. equinox
15. bulgogi
16. niminy-piminy
17. evo-devo
18. wootz
19. pampootie
20. boondoggle

animal scramble

Read the clue for each puzzle and then unscramble the letters to reveal the name of the animal. Finally, use the letters from the highlighted spaces to complete the final puzzle.

1 This mammal has been domesticated in Peru and is often used for transportation, as well as for its wool.

PLAAAC

_ _ _ _ ▪ _

2 This pouched marsupial may be known for hopping, but it can also swim and crawl!

BWLALAY

_ ▪ _ _ _ _ _

3 This slow-moving reptile's life-span is longer than a human's, with the oldest living specimen estimated to be over 190 years old.

SIOTETRO

▪ _ _ _ _ _ _ _

4 These horned mountain climbers can run up to 45 miles per hour.

BEIX

_ _ ▪ _

5 The name of this fish species is often used as part of an exclamation — it follows the word "holy."

KMLEERAC

_ _ _ _ _ ▪ _ _

6 This striking mammal shares its features with several others, including giraffes and zebras.

POIKA

_ _ _ ▪ _

7 Males of this imposing species of monkey look a lot like they're wearing masks.

DLAILMNR

_ _ _ _ _ ▪ _ _

games

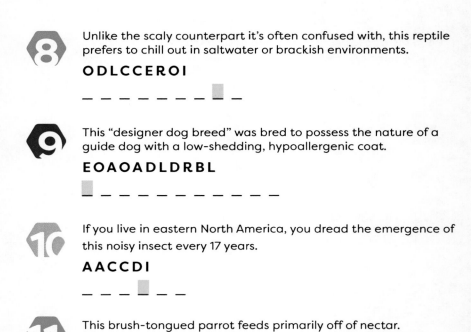

Unlike the scaly counterpart it's often confused with, this reptile prefers to chill out in saltwater or brackish environments.

ODLCCEROI

_ _ _ _ _ _ ▮ _

This "designer dog breed" was bred to possess the nature of a guide dog with a low-shedding, hypoallergenic coat.

EOAOADLDRBL

▮ _ _ _ _ _ _ _ _ _ _

If you live in eastern North America, you dread the emergence of this noisy insect every 17 years.

AACCDI

_ _ _ ▮ _ _

This brush-tongued parrot feeds primarily off of nectar.

KRETELOI

_ _ ▮ _ _ _ _ _

Use the highlighted letters from each answer to complete the final puzzle!

_ _ _ _ _ _ _ _ _ _ _

55

word ladders

Change one letter in each line to get from the first
2024 Words of the Champions word to the last!

The first one is done for you. Can you do the rest?

W A N D
W A R D
W A R P
W A S P

1

P R O N E
_ _ _ _ _
T R O V E

2

O U S T E R
_ _ _ _ _ _
M I S T E R

3

B R I C K
_ _ _ _ _
B L I N K

4

S L A B
_ _ _ _
_ _ _ _
S P R Y

5

D A I S Y
_ _ _ _ _
_ _ _ _ _
_ _ _ _ _
F O L L Y

6

F I E
_ _ _
_ _ _
E W E

7

W A M B L E
_ _ _ _ _ _
_ _ _ _ _ _
_ _ _ _ _ _
_ _ _ _ _ _
G I G G L E

DAFT

_ _ _ _

_ _ _ _

_ _ _ _

_ _ _ _

DIVA

PEAT

_ _ _ _

_ _ _ _

_ _ _ _

_ _ _ _

AWRY

one last
challenge!

THORN

_ _ _ _ _

_ _ _ _ _

_ _ _ _ _

_ _ _ _ _

_ _ _ _ _

_ _ _ _ _

_ _ _ _ _

WRING

crossword puzzle
people and their work

across

1 performs miscellaneous tasks (as in a home or public building) (8)

3 investigates complaints in an official capacity (9)

5 handles lighting and electrical needs on a motion picture set (6)

6 plans and supervises projects in a technical field (8)

8 fights with their fists professionally : a boxer (8)

10 manages an opera company (10)

13 sells old things, such as rare old books (11)

14 organizes economic venture - for example, by starting new businesses (12)

down

2 prepares and sells medicines (10)

4 works with masses of numerical data (12)

5 studies handwriting (12)

7 practices a branch of medicine that focuses on structural integrity of the tissue (9)

9 invests large amounts of money (9)

11 sells houses and other such properties, as well as land (7)

12 handles customer payments (as in a store) (7)

attitudes & emotions

```
A P P R E H E N S I V E S U U W
I Y U D O M I N E E R I N G X N
S D J D A T F I F K E O T L C C
C T X C L J J B Q Q P U T H K A
D I S T R A U G H T E I A K J N
D Q I Z B U B B L Y N B F D X D
F O C K V V J U M T T A W B V I
D U W H G L I G G L A I K T N D
Y O R N T A Q N U Q N C N J T R
T F J U C Y Q F D Q T A W N O Y
L T K J A A T O A I L M A V L T
U P U C K I S H Q I C I P R N H
X V N B E R B T B S L T U O M B
V M V C N E M U C A I S I U B Y
L U E W W T J H V Q I R D V Q S
W D C H A R I S T M A T I C E J
```

apprehensive	jubilant
bubbly	puckish
candid	repentant
deceitful	surly
distraught	valiant
domineering	vindictive
downcast	

Made in United States
North Haven, CT
11 June 2024

53509977R00033